Giant Pandas

by Marcia S. Freeman

Consulting Editor:
Gail Saunders-Smith, Ph.D.

Consultant:
Don Middleton, Member
International Association for
Bear Research and Management

Pebble Books

an imprint of Capstone Press
Mankato, Minnesota

Pebble Books are published by Capstone Press
818 North Willow Street, Mankato, Minnesota 56001
http://www.capstone-press.com

Library of Congress Cataloging-in-Publication Data
Freeman, Marcia S. (Marcia Sheehan), 1937–
        Giant pandas/by Marcia S. Freeman.
        p. cm.—(Bears)
        Includes bibliographical references and index.
        Summary: Simple text and photographs describe the appearance, food, and homes of the
giant panda.
        ISBN 0-7368-0098-0
        1. Giant panda—Juvenile literature. [1. Giant panda. 2. Pandas.] I. Title. II. Series.
QL737.C214.F74 1999
599.789—DC21   98-19959
                                                                      CIP
                                                                       AC

Note to Parents and Teachers

Books in this series may be used together in comparative activities to investigate
different types of bears. The series supports the national science education
standards for units on the diversity and unity of animal life. This book describes
and illustrates the appearance and activities of the giant panda of China. The
photographs support early readers in understanding the text. The sentence
structures offer subtle challenges. This book introduces early readers to
vocabulary used in this subject area. The vocabulary is defined in the Words to
Know section. Early readers may need assistance in reading some words and in
using the Table of Contents, Words to Know, Read More, Internet Sites, and
Index/Word List sections of the book.

Table of Contents

Giant pandas have black fur and white fur.

Giant pandas have black fur around their eyes.

Giant pandas have
black fur on their ears.

Giant pandas live in bamboo forests in China.

Giant pandas climb trees.

Giant pandas eat bamboo leaves and bamboo stems.

Giant pandas spend
most of the day eating.

Female giant pandas
have cubs during
summer or autumn.

19

Giant pandas are endangered. Few giant pandas live in the wild.

Words to Know

bamboo—a tall grass with a tough stem

cub—a young bear

endangered—in danger of dying out

female—a person or animal that can give birth or lay eggs

forest—a large area covered with trees and plants

fur—the hairy coat of an animal

leaf—the flat and usually green part of a plant that grows out from a stem

stem—the long part of a plant from which leaves and flowers grow

wild—an area that is in its natural state; giant pandas live in bamboo forests in China.

Read More

Duden, Jane. *The Giant Pandas of China.* Animals of the World. Mankato, Minn.: Hilltop Books, 1998.

Dudley, Karen. *Giant Pandas.* The Untamed World. Austin, Texas: Raintree Steck-Vaughn, 1997.

Feeney, Kathy. *Pandas for Kids.* Wildlife for Kids. Minocqua, Wis.: NorthWord Press, 1997.

Fowler, Allan. *Giant Pandas: Gifts from China.* Rookie Read-About Science. Chicago: Children's Press, 1995.

Internet Sites

All about Pandas
http://www.fonz.org/ppage.htm

Giant Pandas
http://www.nature-net.com/bears/panda.html

Pandas
http://www.fonz.org/ffpanda.htm

Index/Word List

autumn, 19
bamboo, 11, 15
China, 11
cubs, 19
day, 17
ears, 9
eyes, 7

forests, 11
fur, 5, 7, 9
leaves, 15
stems, 15
summer, 19
trees, 13
wild, 21

Word Count: 72
Early-Intervention Level: 9

Editorial Credits
Michelle L. Norstad, editor; Clay Schotzko/Icon Productions, cover designer;
  Sheri Gosewisch, photo researcher

Photo Credits
Animals Animals/Mark Stouffer, 18
Dembinsky Photo Assoc. Inc., 14, 16, 20
Lynn M. Stone, 4, 6, 8, 10, 12
Root Resources/Kenneth W. Fink, cover; Alan G. Nelson, 1